And Then God Made Laughter

YC A YOUNG CHRISTIAN BOOK FOR GIRLS

And Then God Made Laughter

BARBARA DEGROTE-SORENSEN

AUGSBURG Publishing House • Minneapolis

AND THEN GOD MADE LAUGHTER
A Young Christian Book for Girls

Copyright © 1989 Augsburg Publishing House

All rights reserved. Except for brief quotations in critical articles or reviews, no part of this book may be reproduced in any manner without prior written permission from the publisher. Write to: Permissions, Augsburg Publishing House, 426 S. Fifth St., Box 1209, Minneapolis MN 55440.

Scripture quotations unless otherwise noted are from the Holy Bible: New International Version. Copyright 1978 by the New York International Bible Society. Used by permission of Zondervan Bible Publishers.

Scripture quotations marked RSV are from the Revised Standard Version of the Bible, copyright 1946, 1952, and 1971 by the Division of Christian Education of the National Council of Churches.

Photos: CLEO Photography, 24, 90; Roger W. Neal, 38; Skjold Photography, 56, 80, 102.

Library of Congress Cataloging-in-Publication Data

DeGrote-Sorensen, Barbara, 1954–
    And then God made laughter : a young Christian book for girls / Barbara DeGrote-Sorensen.
      p.   cm.
    ISBN 0-8066-2383-7
    1. Girls—Prayer-books and devotions—English. 2. Christian life—Lutheran authors. I. Titles.
BV4860.D43   1989
248.8'2—dc19   89-384
                                                                             CIP

Manufactured in the U.S.A.   APH 10-0346

1 2 3 4 5 6 7 8 9 0 1 2 3 4 5 6 7 8 9

*For my children
Katie, Jill, and Reed
because I love them*

Contents

About This Book	11
And for This I Gave Up a Week at Aunt Elaine's?	13
Can't You Take a Joke?	25
Shop 'Til You Drop	39
The Building with Broken Windows	53
One Bottle of Pop on the Wall	67
The Killer Instinct	81
For Grandma	87
Here's Looking at You	99

About This Book

What's the best time you've ever had? What made it so much fun? The people you were with? The place? Maybe you reached a goal. Won a game. Or scored a perfect paper on your math quiz. Did you ever have fun when you weren't expecting to, or have a really rotten time when you thought it was going to be the best? Fun can be terribly unfunny sometimes.

Every day, whether you're aware of it or not, you're probably getting a lot of advice about how to have the ultimate "good time."

"Hey, fun! That's what it's all about!"
"It takes money to have fun."
"Buy this! Try this! Be cool!"
"Party, party, party!"
"Are we having fun yet?"

Let's get one thing straight. Fun is only fun when *you* think it's fun. Not because of what some group in school says or what some TV commercial or video tries to tell you. And sometimes what you think is fun isn't at all what others may call fun.

It's hard sometimes to fit in—to know who to follow. Jesus knows it's hard. That's one reason he came, to show us the way. And he said it very clearly: "I am the light of the world. He who follows me will not walk in darkness, but will have the light of life" (John 8:1). Fun means walking in the light.

And Then God Made Laughter

Can you be Christian, a Christ-follower, and still have fun? You bet, because you've got the best of both worlds. You've got the world God created for you and you've got a God who really cares about you.

Who created the laugh, the giggle, the smile, and the chuckle? Who created the joke? Not Peewee Herman—God! Could anyone have created both the giraffe and the turtle without a sense of humor?

God wants you to grow and enjoy your life. God also wants you to know what's fun and what's fake. There's a world of difference.

The girls in this book are just like you. They like having fun. But like you, they sometimes get confused about what's fun and what isn't:

- Am I too old to have fun with my family?
- When is a joke not a joke?
- What's the big deal about partying?
- Can I have fun without getting in trouble?

You can read this book all alone in your room or out loud with your Sunday school class. You'll find Bible verses to help lead you into the stories, while the prayers and action ideas bring the stories into your own life.

I hope you have fun reading this book. I had fun writing it. It will make you smile a little and laugh a lot. It may make you think some, too.

What's fun—what's fake? Think about it.

A friend—
BARBARA DEGROTE-SORENSEN

"And . . . everything that moves . . . went forth by families out of the ark."
—Genesis 8:19 RSV

•

"It's a deflated basketball, squished between two hamburger buns with zits!"
—Ricka

And for This I Gave Up a Week at Aunt Elaine's?

1

Carna Plummet slouched lower in the backseat of the family's slightly dented—but not too embarrassingly—Toyota wagon. It hadn't been her idea to go to the drive-in for supper, but her mom had gotten an unexpected bonus in the mail and decided to treat the family.

"The family" included one slightly in-shape dad who was still proud of the fact he had "most" of his hair. That, Carna always said, was a matter of opinion.

Her mother had her hair in a long ponytail that hung past her shoulders. She was one of the few moms, Carna noticed, who hadn't gone for one of those short, practical cuts mothers are always getting.

Carna thought it was kind of neat to call her mother by her first name. She had tried it out once on "Joannie," but the results were not encouraging.

That left only "Reeeka," a nickname despised by Carna's younger sister, but of enormous personal value to Carna when Ricka, as she was supposed to be called, seemed to be coming out ahead in some argument or another.

Joannie thought they had a "cute" family. She was always saying, "Isn't that cute!" or "Aren't we cute!"—especially when the family did something together.

Cute was not the word Carna preferred to call these family outings. *Embarrassing* was more like it. And this drive-in idea was definitely more embarrassing than cute.

"We're here!" Ricka announced, bouncing up and down in the seat in front of Carna.

Carna preferred the far backseat of the car. It made family outings almost bearable—especially those long rides to Aunt Elaine's that the family managed to make at least once a summer.

Carna slouched lower yet as she checked out the scene at the drive-in. Mostly high school kids with their dates or families with little kids. No one Carna recognized or no one who would recognize her. "Safe!" Carna breathed.

"Let me order! Let me order!" Ricka screamed

And for This I Gave Up a Week at Aunt Elaine's?

as the eight-year-old unbuckled her seatbelt and scooted to the window nearest the intercom.

"Isn't that cute," Joannie murmured sweetly. "Now just wait until Mommy and Daddy figure out what they want, honey."

Carna felt a faint growl in her stomach as the rest of the family squinted at the menu printed outside their window.

"How about a teen basket?" Joannie asked back to Carna.

Carna sat up. "What is it?" she asked, squinting back into the glare from the car window.

"It's a deflated basketball, squished between two hamburger buns with zits!" Ricka giggled and then roared at her joke.

Carna slouched back down to her original position.

"Now, Ricka!" Joannie warned with a glint in her eye that could be taken either as a mother who was mad or a mother who was trying not to laugh.

She's trying not to laugh. I can tell she's trying not to smile. Joannie really thinks it's cute. I can't believe it.

"Hey, Mom!" Carna called over Ricka's hysterical giggles. "Reeeka wants a baby burger basket. Something bitty for the baby."

"Mother!" Ricka protested.

"Carna!" Joannie said with the same glint in her eye.

Well, at least Joannie's being fair about it, Carna thought, tossing a disgusted look at Ricka who was

15

And Then God Made Laughter

now leaning halfway out the window waiting to yell everyone's order into the speaker.

"OK, Ricka," Mr. Plummet began. "We'll have two California burgers—"

"Two California Burgers!" Ricka screamed into the speaker.

"One teen basket," Mr. Plummet continued.

"One teen basket," Ricka screamed louder yet.

Carna noticed a few people were beginning to stare out their car windows at the racket. Carna pretended to drop something on the car floor and bent down and out of sight as long as she could.

"What to drink, Carna?" Joannie called back. "Carna?"

"Milk," Carna called back weakly, quite out of air from being bent over for that long.

"Milk!" Ricka continued at high volume. Carna sat up when the carhop arrived with their order. She was in the middle of her third bite when the big announcement came. . . .

Carna's prayer: *Dear God, I thought surprises were supposed to be fun! Amen.*

And for This I Gave Up a Week at Aunt Elaine's?

2

"What do you mean we're not going to Aunt Elaine's this year?" Ricka whined.

Joannie had turned almost fully around from her place in the front. "Now, Ricka, I said there was good news and bad news. I haven't told you the good news yet," she explained to the the sniffling Ricka.

If not going to Aunt Elaine's is the bad news, I can hardly wait to hear the good news, Carna mused.

Going to Aunt Elaine's was kind of a family tradition. At least, the Plummet family had visited Aunt Elaine every summer since Carna was a baby.

Aunt Elaine really wasn't an aunt. She was a great-aunt—Joannie's great-aunt—which made her really old. Carna remembered as a little girl Aunt Elaine's Kool-Aid always had too much water in it and she always served a vegetable with every meal, even breakfast! It had been fun to explore Aunt Elaine's old house for secret treasures or old letters and stuff. Ricka still loved it. But Carna was beginning to be a little bored with it all. Aunt Elaine was nice enough. That wasn't the problem. It's just that Aunt Elaine's wasn't Carna's idea of an exciting vacation. Besides, the six-hour car ride with Ricka almost killed her. A person can only listen to "100 bottles of pop on the wall" so many times.

"Mommy's bonus was a lot more than I expected this year," Joannie continued. Visions of Aunt Elaine's began to vanish from Carna's head as she thought of far-off places she'd rather go during summer break.

That's it! Mom's going to take us all to . . . to Florida . . . Disney World. Maybe Tahiti!

Carna wasn't sure where Tahiti was, but she had seen a travel brochure on it once at the dentist's office.

Tahiti. Carna began to write her back-to-school English composition in her head. *"What I Did On My Summer Vacation" by Carna Plummet.*

". . . And well, Dad and I have talked it over," Joannie continued, "and we would like to take the whole family camping for two weeks. Just the four of us! Well, what do you think?" Joannie said, fairly beaming with her news.

Visions of Tahiti soon joined Aunt Elaine as the truth of what Joannie had just announced began to sink into Carna's thoughts.

Camping for two weeks. In a tent. With Reeeka!

"Mother!" Carna whined.

"Now, Carna," Joannie piped, "you'll have a lot of fun. Before long you'll have a job—"

"Or a boyfriend," Mr. Plummet laughed, trying to kid Carna out of her mood.

"Now, John," Joannie stopped long enough to give her husband one of her "I'll handle this" looks. "Anyway," Joannie continued, "before long you won't be able to come with us on family outings. I know we'll just have a great time!"

"Do I have to sleep on Ricka's side of the tent?"

And for This I Gave Up a Week at Aunt Elaine's?

Carna asked, starting to be practical about the situation.

"We'll work something out," Mr. Plummet said. "Isn't anybody going to ask where we're going?"

"Where we going?" Ricka shouted, almost climbing over the seat to see the map Joannie was pulling from the glove compartment.

"OK! OK!" Joannie laughed. "We'll start off on a Friday and spend our first night at. . . ."

Two weeks in a tent with the family! Carna groaned inwardly. *How cute.*

There was no escape. Not unless Carna came up with a job or a boyfriend really quick. She was stuck and there was nothing she could do about it.

Carna's prayer: *Dear God, if I have to go could you please give Ricka laryngitis at least during the car rides? And God, is it really possible to have fun with your family? Amen.*

And Then God Made Laughter

3

It had rained since the Plummet family pulled out of their driveway at 5:00 that morning, headed for "a real family adventure," to quote Joannie. It was still raining as the family wagon and camper pulled into the first state park campground on their two-week agenda.

"This is it! Gooseberry State Park," Joannie announced, peering through the downpour at the sign at the gate.

"You people have a real nice time, now," the park ranger said as Carna counted the waterdrops dripping off his nose.

"Hey!" Ricka suddenly popped up, "Gooseberry Park! Get it! Goose-berry?" Ricka made a sudden attack on Carna and gave her a hefty pinch.

"Gotcha!" Ricka screamed in delight. "Don't you get it? Goose-berry?" Ricka prepared for Carna's return attack by piling up pillows and other stuff around herself.

"Grow up, Reeeka!" Carna said in her most self-controlled, adult-sounding voice.

Carna had figured out the only way to silence Ricka was to not participate. That meant no yelling. No fighting. No wisecracks. Nothing. Just maturity. It worked every time.

Ricka wilted as Carna kept herself busy collecting her odds and ends. "You're no fun anymore," Ricka whined from her side of the seat.

And for This I Gave Up a Week at Aunt Elaine's?

Ricka's words settled into a hollow little lump in Carna's stomach and she almost started to apologize. Almost, but not quite.

"Come on, you guys," Mr. Plummet said in his most enthusiastic voice. "We're going to need everyone's cooperation to pull this one off." Turning to Joannie, who was busy handing out raingear and encouragement, he asked, "Can you believe it's been raining all day?"

"Great, isn't it," Joannie said, still smiling. She had been smiling the entire trip. Carna began to wonder what was really going on. No one could be that happy. Especially on a 350-mile car ride.

"That's your mother," Mr. Plummet laughed. "The eternal optimist!"

"Opti—what?" Ricka said, recovering from Carna's putdown.

"It means she's always seeing the good in something. Even rain and long rides," Carna explained patiently to Ricka.

"Oh," Ricka giggled. "I thought she was sick or something."

Mr. Plummet laughed again. "Well, some people think Joannie's a little too—"

Joannie's eyebrows shot up. "Too what?"

"Too good to be true," Mr. Plummet finished. "But that's one of the things I love about your mother, girls. She's fun to be with." Mr. Plummet leaned over and planted a big kiss on Joannie's face.

"Why, thank you, John," Joannie said. "That was very nice."

21

And Then God Made Laughter

"I'm a nice guy!" Mr. Plummet said, opening the van door and jumping into the downpour.

Carna began to feel a little sick. Not the kind of sick you get from riding with Ricka in the backseat for seven hours, but the kind of sick you get when you realize maybe you've done something wrong.

You're no fun anymore. Ricka's words settled deeper into Carna's thoughts. *That's what I love about your mother. She's fun to be with! Fun to be with! Fun to be with!* Carna pulled her rain poncho over her head and slid out of the van and into the rain.

"Geronimo!" Ricka yelled as she jumped from the seat to the soggy ground below.

Carna seized the moment. "Gotcha!" she yelled, goosing Ricka. "Goose-berry Park? Goose? Get it?" Carna laughed at Ricka's speechless expression.

"Unfair!" Ricka yelled, her face breaking into a smile.

"All's fair in love and war!" Carna yelled back as she began to chase Ricka around the car.

Joannie stood in the rain as Mr. Plummet cranked open the trailer and the girls scampered in.

"Aren't they cute!" Joannie said as she watched the girls' antics.

"Not as cute as you!" Mr. Plummet said with a wink.

"Hey!" Joannie suddenly yelled.

"Gotcha!" Mr. Plummet laughed back. "Gooseberry Park? Goose? Get it?"

"Prepare to defend yourself," Joannie said, diving into the trailer.

22

And for This I Gave Up a Week at Aunt Elaine's?

"All hands on deck! Pull up the anchor!" Mr. Plummet joked, shutting the door and leaving the rain pattering on the window.

"One hundred bottles of pop on the wall," Ricka sang as the others covered their ears and groaned.

Joannie's prayer: *Lord, thank you for this family. Help us use this vacation time to really get to know each other. There's nothing more fun than spending time with the people you love. That goes for you too, Lord. Amen.*

Action idea: Plan an outing with your family. Go out of your way to be fun to be with.

And Then God Made Laughter

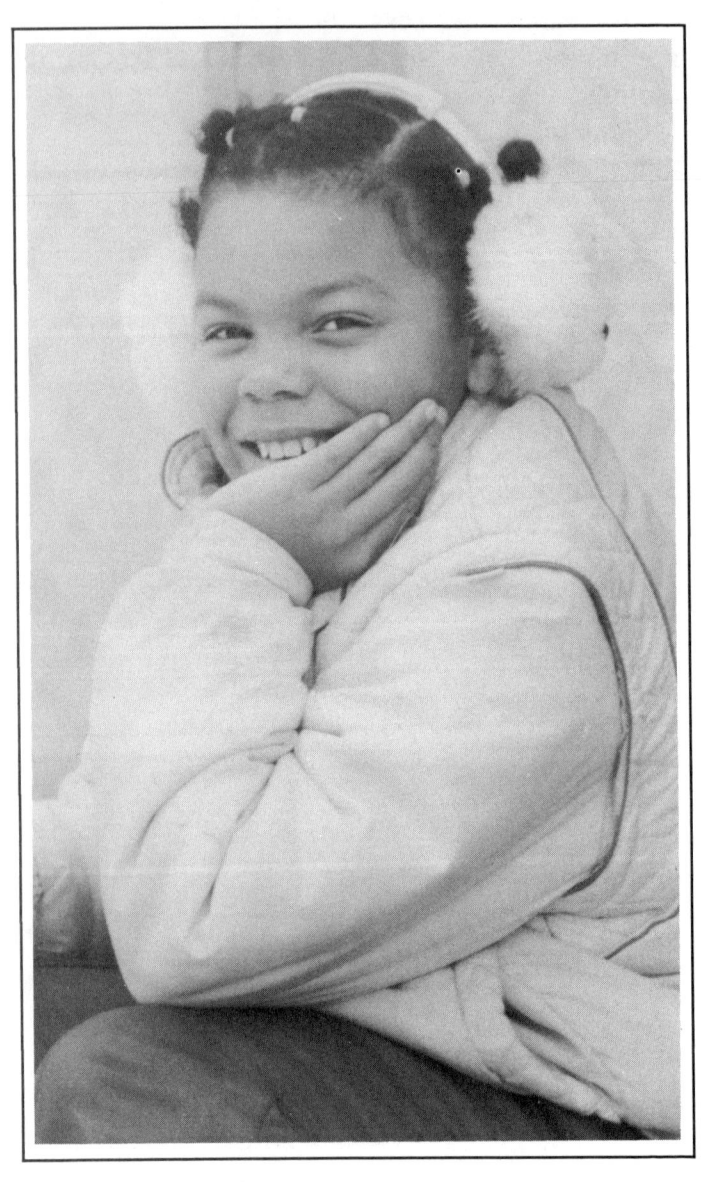

"For he never thought of doing a kindness."
—Psalm 109:16

•

*"It's time to give him a taste
of his own medicine!"
—Jonathan*

Can't You Take a Joke?

1

"And remember, your weekly book reports are due tomorrow. No excuses!" Ms. Gerhard announced. "OK, that's all. Stay in your seats until the bell. And Chris Richards, I need to see you after class."

"Wonder what he's done now?" Erin whispered across the aisle to Jill.

"You know Chris," Jill whispered in return. "He's always getting in trouble."

"Yeah, and always at someone else's expense," Erin murmured. "Did you hear he pulled out Jonathan's chair in science and they think he might have bruised his backbone. He had to have X-rays!"

"Real funny," Jill said. "What's he trying to prove anyway?"

"Beats me. But Mom says he's just trying to get

And Then God Made Laughter

attention. Next thing you know he'll be putting tacks on people's chairs!"

"Ouch!" A loud yell came from the back of the room as Danny Peters jumped up and started pulling at the back of his jeans.

"What's the matter? Got ants in your pants?" Chris Richards laughed, looking around the room to see who was watching. Danny's face turned bright red as he sat back down in his seat but not without first checking his chair.

"Class!" Ms. Gerhard exclaimed. "That's enough—" But the final bell rang and her comments were lost to the commotion of 30 people trying to get through one door at the same time.

"No one's safe," Erin said to the small group of kids who had gathered at the store across the street from the junior high. "Chris will do anything for a laugh."

Jonathan scowled as he rubbed his backside "You're telling me! One moment I'm standing up and the next—" Jonathan gestured towards the floor—"I'm wiped out and everyone's laughing."

"Especially Chris Richards!" Erin piped in. "I don't think it's funny to go around embarrassing other people."

"Chris Richards does," someone in the next booth leaned over to join the conversation.

"That's just it," Jonathan insisted. "He's probably having a good laugh right now! Ha. Ha. Ha. I say we give him a taste of his own medicine."

Can't You Take a Joke?

"Shhh!" Jill lowered her voice. "Here he comes. Pretend you don't see him. Maybe he'll get the idea."

"Hey guys!" Chris yelled from the door.

"So much for ignoring him," Erin groaned as Chris pulled a chair up to their table.

Chris laughed. "Hey, you should have heard Ms. Gerhard today. I've never seen her so mad. You'd think I'd committed murder or something!"

"Ah, yeah, right," Jonathan said, standing up. "Anybody want anything? I'm getting a Cherry 7-Up."

"Gummy bears," Erin ordered, handing Jonathan some change.

"Same," Jill said.

Chris jumped up suddenly. "Hey! This one's on me. You know, a little apology gift for that accident in science."

Jonathan glared at Chris. "An accident—right. You did it on purpose!"

"Well, let me make it up to you. Really. I insist," Chris said over his shoulder as he headed for the counter.

Erin shook her head. "Amazing! He's actually doing something nice for a change."

"I don't trust him," Jonathan said, still glaring at the retreating Chris. "He's got his back towards us. I say he's up to something."

Chris soon returned with the order. "For you, my friend," he said, handing Jonathan a styrofoam cup filled with pop and ice. "A peace offering."

And Then God Made Laughter

Jill and Erin exchanged puzzled glances as they opened their bags of gummy bears.

Jonathan looked at his glass long and hard before he picked it up and took a long drink. Pop dribbled down his chin and onto his jeans, leaving his lap wet and his face red.

"Jonathan! Your cup!" Jill exclaimed, throwing a dozen paper napkins on the table. "It's got a hole in it!"

Jonathan picked up the cup and tilted it slightly. Pop dripped out of a small hole Chris had neatly poked into the side of the styrofoam just under the rim. The dribble glass. An old trick.

Jonathan jumped up and glared at Chris who was holding his sides as he laughed and pointed at Jonathan.

"Great, huh?" Chris managed to say as he gasped for air. "My older—brother taught me—that one!"

"You—I'll get you for this!" Jonathan roared as he headed for the boy's bathroom.

"What's wrong with him? Can't he take a joke?" Chris laughed again. "It's only pop."

Erin and Jill dumped the rest of their gummy bears on the table, stood up, and headed for the door. A few boys gathered around Chris's table and began to joke back and forth.

Jonathan joined his friends outside. Jill noticed that he had tied his jean jacket around his waist to hide the wet spot on the front of his pants.

"That's it!" Jonathan said as he joined his friends. "No more Mr. Nice Guy from me."

Can't You Take a Joke?

"Well, at least he bought the pop," Jill said, trying to improve the situation.

"Yeah, right. Some peace offering!" Jonathan smirked. "Well, if Chris Richards wants war, he's got it. Now who wants in on the plan?"

Jill's prayer: Dear God, please do something about Chris Richards before Jonathan or somebody else does. It's not safe around here anymore. Amen.

2

Jill felt an uneasy feeling in her stomach as Jonathan told them his plan of revenge.

"OK," Jonathan began. "First we have to win him over. Get him to trust us."

"Yeah, let him think all is forgiven," Danny Peters cut in.

"Then we ask him to go to the mall with us," Jonathan continued slowly.

"Why the mall?" Erin asked.

"Why the mall?" Jonathan repeated. "Because the mall is at least three miles out of town. It'll take him forever to walk back."

"Walk!" Jill said with surprise. "It's the middle of winter."

"That's right." Jonathan's eyes narrowed as he contemplated the half-frozen Chris trudging back to town.

"But don't you think that's dangerous?" Jill continued. "What if he doesn't make it. What if he gets—"

"Oh, quit being such a softy, Jill," Erin said, jabbing her friend with her elbow. "Chris deserves it. Some of his practical jokes have been dangerous, too. And I don't see him feeling too sorry about them."

The rest of the kids murmured their approval.

"OK! Let's do it then," Jonathan summed up the meeting. "We tell Chris to meet us at the mall this Saturday. My mom will drive if you need a ride.

Can't You Take a Joke?

Then we just take off. Leave him stranded. Let's see if he can take a joke as well as he dishes them out."

"And we can watch him from the second floor!" Danny gloated. "I wonder how long he'll wait until he knows he's been left!"

"But what if he won't come?" Jill asked, still not sure she wanted in on Jonathan's little practical joke.

"That's up to you and Erin," Jonathan said matter-of-factly.

Jill jerked her head around to look at Erin. "Why us?" she demanded, suddenly feeling more responsibility then she cared to have.

"Because he likes you," Jonathan grinned. "It's perfect. Betrayed by love."

Jill felt her tonsils hit her toes. "And just how do you know he likes me?" she demanded, quite aware that all the kids were watching Jonathan and her as they worked out this last detail.

"You're about the only one who doesn't know," Jonathan said with a grin. "You know what they say, 'Love is blind.' Come on, Jill. It'll be great; you'll see. You're the only person he'll trust. You're the only one he hasn't played a joke on, right? You have no motive!"

Jill still couldn't believe it. Chris Richards liked her. And now she was supposed to betray him. *Why me!* Jill complained to herself as the group broke up and headed toward their morning classes. Jill was the last one to leave. Somehow she couldn't shake the uneasy feeling that all was not right. Jonathan's practical joke didn't sound funny to her. It just sounded mean. And she wasn't sure anymore that she really wanted a part of it.

Jill's prayer: *When does a joke stop being funny, Lord? Amen.*

Can't You Take a Joke?

3

Danny, Jonathan, Erin, and Jill peered over the balcony wall of the second level of Crestwood Mall and down to the first floor fountain.

"Are you sure he's coming?" Jonathan asked Jill for the third time.

"I told you before," Jill said nervously. "10:30, Saturday morning, by the fountain. And quit asking me if he's going to show up. I hope he doesn't. I don't like this great plan of yours. It's mean."

"Well, la dee da!" Jonathan said, glancing once more to the floor below. "Sounds like you like Chris as much as he's supposed to like you."

Jonathan glanced at his watch one more time. "And you told him we'd give him a ride home, right?"

"Give her a break will you, Jonathan!" Erin cut in. "And what do you mean 'as much as Chris is supposed to like Jill.' I thought you said he *did* like her?"

Jill glanced at Erin and then back to Jonathan. "Yeah! You said I was the only one he would trust. 'Betrayed by love,' remember?" Jill reminded Jonathan of his speech from the day before.

Jonathan cleared his throat. "Well, OK, so I stretched it a bit. But you are the only one that he hasn't played a joke on yet. And you did get him to say he'd come today. So what's the difference?"

And Then God Made Laughter

Jill's eyes blazed with anger. "So you lied!" she said accusingly.

"Ah, well, not exactly," Jonathan began.

"Hey! There he is!" Danny announced, pointing to a small figure in a red windbreaker.

"Are you sure?" Jill asked, peering over the edge, trying to get a better look.

"Get down!" Jonathan whispered. "He'll see you!"

"It's him, all right," Erin said from her post behind the potted plant. "Now what do we do?"

Jonathan grinned mischievously. "Nothing. Absolutely nothing. We just watch him."

Jill was already squirming. Jonathan's plan to pay Chris back had lost its earlier appeal.

It's my fault, Jill thought, turning away from the rest of the group. *I'm the one who got him to come. I'm the one he trusted.* Jill remembered the funny look on Chris's face when she had asked him to join her and a few others at the mall. He had looked, well, happy. Jill began to feel more and more guilty as she watched Chris pace back and forth on the floor below.

"Revenge! Sweet revenge!" Jonathan gloated as he watched the pacing Chris. "Three miles to town. Three miles of cold, lonely highway!"

"You're sick!" Jill said, turning on Jonathan. "You're as bad as Chris!"

"The ultimate put-down," Jonathan shot back. "Look, Jill, if you don't like this, you're welcome to leave. You've done your part."

Can't You Take a Joke?

"And walk back to town?" Jill said. "You said your mother would give us a ride."

Jonathan just smiled curtly and continued to watch Chris below.

One hour later, after one foot-long hotdog and two trips to the men's room, Chris was still waiting.

"This is great," Danny hooted. "Wait 'til we tell everybody at school that Chris Richards waited over an hour for us and we were watching all the time. This should take him down a notch or two."

"I'm bored," Erin announced. "What time did you say your mother was coming?"

"In about 10 minutes. And then it's good-bye mall and good-bye Chris! I told you this was a great plan! Let's go. Takes at least 10 minutes to walk to the south door. That's where we're supposed to meet my mom."

Erin, Danny, and Jonathan gathered their stuff and started down the hallway.

"Hey, Jill," Erin stopped and looked back at her friend. "Aren't you coming?"

Jill took one more look at the red windbreaker below and took a deep breath. "No thanks," she said calmly. "I think I'll walk."

"Oh, come off it. Well, fine. Suit yourself," Jonathan sneered as he walked away. "It's a long ways back," he yelled, turning around. "Girls!" he muttered to Danny, who had stopped to look in a store window. "I'll never understand them."

"If Jill stays, so do I," Erin suddenly announced.

And Then God Made Laughter

"This was a dumb idea. All it did was make you feel big!" Erin snapped at Jonathan.

"What? Give me a break. Somebody's got to teach Chris a lesson. He asked for it. If you baby him he'll keep doing it. Let him learn the hard way," Jonathan said.

"Why don't you come and be his friend? Maybe then he'll stop doing stuff," Erin shot back.

"Forget it. No way. See you guys later. C'mon Danny." The boys walked away.

"Thanks," Jill said to Erin as they took the escalator to the first floor.

"Don't mention it," Erin said, grinning. "It was—"

"I know," Jill cut in, "a dumb idea."

"Hey! Hey, you guys!" Chris's voice rang across the crowded mall. "Where you been? I just about started walking!"

"Anybody got a quarter for a phone call?" Jill asked, digging in her purse. "We're gonna need a ride."

"A ride?" Chris asked. "I thought you said somebody's mom was picking us up."

"They left," Erin interrupted. "And be glad they did. We'll explain later. In the meantime, we need to talk. Sit."

Chris Richards sat.

"They were going to leave me here?" he asked when Jill and Erin finished.

"They did leave you here," Erin laughed. Jill went to the pay phone.

Can't You Take a Joke?

"I guess it was because of the tack and the pop and—" Chris began.

"And don't forget the chair in science," Erin insisted.

Jill returned. "My brother said he'd come in 40 minutes. We're supposed to meet him by the main entrance."

Chris nervously twisted his red windbreaker. He spoke softly. "Erin. Jill. You guys, I really am sorry. I mean it. Thanks for staying."

"Oh, forget it," Erin grinned, slapping him on the back. "But if I ever see a tack on my chair—"

"Moi? Me?" Chris perked up. "A thing of the past. You are looking at a new man!"

Jill and Erin laughed as Chris tore down the hall ahead of them.

"Do you believe him?" Jill asked.

"We'll just have to wait and see," Erin said, shaking her head. "But I wouldn't sit down for a while without checking my chair."

Jill's prayer: Dear God, don't ask me why I stuck up for Chris. But I'm glad I did. A joke's never funny when somebody gets hurt. Thanks for giving me the chance to make things right. Amen.

Action idea: Borrow a joke book from your school library and share a couple of the best ones with your family or friends.

And Then God Made Laughter

"Forgive us our debts..."
—Matthew 6:12

•

"How am I going to pay for all this!
—*Leigh*

Shop 'Til You Drop

1

"This is addicting!" Jan yelled to Leigh as she grabbed a size 7 off the rack and headed for the dressing room.

"You're telling me!" Leigh yelled back over the crowd of people taking advantage of one of Peabody's biggest sale days.

"Sorry, miss," said the sales clerk, looking up from Leigh's growing pile of clothes, hangers, and other paraphernalia, "only three items allowed in the dressing room at one time."

Leigh looked down at three pairs of pants, five sweaters, two skirts, and the $45 blouse she knew she could never afford but wanted to try on anyway.

"I'll hang them here for you if you wish," the sales clerk suggested. "Just exchange them when you're done."

And Then God Made Laughter

Leigh reluctantly handed over all but two of the sweaters and the off-white jeans. *Only three items! How is a person supposed to find anything when you can't even try it on,* Leigh complained to herself as she headed for one of the back rooms.

"Leigh! Over here!" Jan called, sticking her head out from behind one of the curtained off areas. "This place is a zoo. Want to share a room?"

Leigh darted into Jan's room before the sales clerk had a chance to catch her.

"What did you find?" Jan asked, wiggling her way into the size 7 jeans she had chosen from the sale table.

"Too much," Leigh sighed. "I'm already in debt to everyone in my family including Heidi, and she's only seven."

Jan sucked in her stomach and tried to zip the front zipper. Half-way up, she ran out of air and collapsed onto the bench next to the full-length mirror.

"Maybe if you laid on the floor," Leigh suggested.

"Never mind," Jan sighed. "At home I lay upside down on the stairs so my weight goes to the upper half of my body and I still can't fit into a 7. Two weeks until school starts and I'm still 10 pounds away from anything that resembles skinny."

Leigh gave her friend a sympathetic smile, zipped up the jeans she was trying on, and reached for one of the sweaters.

Jan was not so easily consoled.

"It isn't fair," she half-complained. "You look good in everything. Wish I did!"

Shop 'Til You Drop

Leigh smiled at her own reflection in the mirror. The sweater looked great with the pants.

"I can't decide," Leigh said. "What do you like? The blue or the red?"

"Both!" Janet laughed. "But what does it matter? I thought you said you were broke."

"I am. But I still got Mom's charge card she gave me for Heidi's birthday present. This is such a good buy and—"

"And it *does* look good on you," Jan encouraged. "But won't she get mad? I mean, you've got to pay for it sometime."

Leigh gathered up all three items and handed them to Jan. "I need these. They're perfect!" she stated in a matter-of-fact voice. "Anyway, the bill won't come for two weeks. By then I could save up."

"You!" Jan laughed. "The last time you saved anything was a sack of aluminum cans and we had to fill some of them with rocks just to get $1.50 out of it."

"Don't remind me! I really got bawled out for that one," Leigh lamented her last attempt at obtaining finances. "Besides, I really need these!"

"Right," Jan said with another laugh. "Just like I need another 10 pounds. Don't call me when your parents hit the ceiling!"

Leigh signed her name on the dotted line, picked up her packages and waited for Jan to catch up with her.

"We've still got 45 minutes before the last bus. Let's hit some more stores," Leigh suggested to Jan.

And Then God Made Laughter

"But, Leigh—"

Leigh laughed. "Don't worry! I'm just going to browse!"

Jan gave her friend one of her "I don't believe you for a second" looks. "You're hopeless," she sighed to Leigh who was looking at a store across the hall.

"Trust me," Leigh said over her shoulder as she headed down the hall to another crowded department store.

Five stores and three purchases later, a tired Leigh and a half-hysterical Jan slumped down on a hall bench next to the escalator.

"Don't even say it!" Leigh moaned, looking down at the bags at her feet. "I'm hopeless. I'm worse than hopeless; I'm dead. How am I going to pay for all this?"

Leigh's prayer: *Dear God, sometimes it's hard to tell the difference between what I need and what I just want. Help! Amen.*

Shop 'Til You Drop

2

"Leigh!" Mrs. Bourn called from the kitchen. "Would you come here, please."

Something in her mother's voice warned Leigh that this was not going to be a "milk and cookies" conversation. The bill had come.

Mrs. Bourn was seated at the kitchen table surrounded by letters, envelopes, some pens, and her usual cup of tea. In her hand dangled the August statement from her major credit card.

"Ah, I can explain," Leigh began, not exactly sure what she was going to say.

"I certainly hope so!" Mrs. Bourn said with more than a touch of anger in her voice. "$157.49! Leigh! How could you?"

Leigh swallowed hard. She knew the bill was going to be high, but $157! It would take months to save that much.

"I'll pay it back, Mom," Leigh promised.

"I should say you will, young lady," Mrs. Bourn said, still scowling at the bill. "Starting right now, I will be keeping most of your allowance, and any baby-sitting money must be turned immediately over to me until you have paid for every cent of this!"

"But Mother—," Leigh complained.

"And furthermore, you will return what you can for a refund immediately," Mrs. Bourn continued, thumping the table with her fist.

Leigh stood silently and picked at the edge of the

And Then God Made Laughter

table. "I can't," she mumbled. "It was all on sale. No returns." Leigh paused. "I'm really sorry, Mom. I just couldn't stop!"

"I see," Mrs. Bourn said in a voice that meant she did not see and was not about to see. "In that case, there will be no more charging—" Mrs. Bourn stopped. "Make that, no more *shopping* until this bill is paid in full. Is that understood?"

"What?" Leigh asked. "No shopping?"

"Not even looking," her mother said firmly.

Leigh felt weak in her knees. This was worse than she ever expected. She expected the charging privileges to be taken away. But not shopping! "But Mom, I promise not to do it anymore. I said I was sorry," she protested.

"That's enough. I don't want to hear any more. No shopping until you pay for this. Is that understood?"

"Yes," Leigh said, starting to feel kind of sick.

Leigh sniffled. Then with a gasp she chuckled, "I'll have withdrawal. My hands will shake. I'll break out in a cold sweat. I'll—"

"Pay the bill," her mother said with a slight smile.

"OK, OK," Leigh said, smiling too, "but what am I going to do for fun in the meantime?"

"I'm sure you'll think of something!" Mrs. Bourn said with a wink as she returned to her bills.

Mrs. Bourn's prayer: Dear Lord, help Leigh find something more important to fill her time with than shopping. Amen.

Shop 'Til You Drop

Leigh's prayer: *Dear God, it's not that I need or even want any more stuff. It's not as much fun when you have to pay for it. Help me find a way to pay Mom back. Amen.*

3

"Well, could have been worse," Jan consoled her friend over the phone that night.

Leigh laughed in disbelief. "I'd like to know how!"

Jan paused. "Well, at least you'll look great, even if you are broke. By the way, how much did you save?"

"$12.80," Leigh responded in a desperate voice. "And that was from two nights with the Alexander twins. That leaves $144.69. It'll take years to pay Mom back everything."

"Maybe not," Jan said. "I just got a phone call from Mrs. Webster. You know, the lady who runs the day care center for retarded kids across from the YMCA?"

"Yeah," Leigh said, recounting her savings she had spilled across her bed.

"She's looking for some kids to come in after school. Two hours a day."

"Great," Leigh remarked with a chuckle. "Volunteer work. What I need is a job!"

"But it is a job. $2 an hour. And we can start on Monday. Now, what do you say?" Jan asked. "I'd do it even if it were volunteer. Those kids are super!"

Leigh sat up straight on her bed. "Did you say pay? But are you sure she wants me? I don't know anything about retarded kids."

"What's to know?" Jan jumped in. "They're kids.

Shop 'Til You Drop

They like to play. And Mrs. Webster asked me to find a couple of friends. So, friend, what do you say?"

"I'll take it!" Leigh jumped off her bed and began sweeping her dollars and change into her hand.

Jan giggled. "I thought you would. One thing I should tell you— *(click)*. Leigh? Leigh?"

But Leigh was already racing down the stairs to tell her mother the good news.

***Leigh's prayer:** Dear God, a job! Thanks! Amen.*

4

"Let's see," Leigh began as she and Jan got off the bus and headed toward their first day of work. "Two dollars an hour at two hours a day makes four dollars a day times five days a week. That makes $20 a week. Only eight weeks and its 'Hello, malls. Hello, shopping!' "

Jan groaned. "Thought you'd be sick of shopping after all the trouble it's caused you."

But Leigh was lost in her daydream. "Oh, to feel the rush of the crowd. The thrill of a bargain. The power of my mother's credit card—"

"No charging!" Jan reminded her.

"The power of my own cash!"

"Well, that's a slight improvement," Jan grinned as she stepped up to Mrs. Webster's front door.

A warm, friendly lady met them at the door. "Hi, Jan!" Mrs. Webster greeted the girls. "And who did you bring with you today?"

"This is Leigh Bourn," Jan said. "She's done a lot of baby-sitting, but not much work with special kids."

"There's not much difference," Mrs. Webster said, smiling at Leigh. "But let's introduce you to the kids. They've been looking forward to your coming."

Mrs. Webster led the girls back through a narrow hallway into a large room at the back of the house. Two other grown-ups looked up at Leigh and Jan

Shop 'Til You Drop

as they entered. At the same time five of the kids descended on the girls, pulling on their legs and hands.

Leigh looked down in disgust. One of the little boys had put two handprints on her new white jeans. The ones she was still paying for.

"Come on, Donny. Snack is over. Let's go wash your hands," Mrs. Webster spoke softly to the little boy. "It's just peanut butter," Mrs. Webster said to Leigh as she picked up the little boy and carried him to the sink.

Leigh looked in horror at the marks on her pants.

"An occupational hazard. I was going to tell you not to overdress. They have a lot of fun here, but it can get a little messy," Jan explained as she began setting up some blocks on the floor. "And by the way, not all of them are trained. You know. You could get a little wet."

Leigh leaned back against the wall. The Alexander kids were always exceptionally neat. The most Leigh had ever had to do was wipe up a spilled glass of milk or some crumbs from the table.

Leigh looked around the room. Most of the kids were playing happily in groups or by themselves. But Leigh noticed one little boy in the corner by himself, rocking back and forth. He appeared to be about five, but Leigh could tell he still wore diapers. His nose was running down his face and he had smeared the snot across his check and into his hair. It was not a pleasant sight.

And Then God Made Laughter

"That's Greggie," Mrs. Webster explained, coming back from the sink with a much cleaner Donnie. "He's mentally retarded and also blind. He just started here a few days ago. Why don't you see if you can get him to play with you."

Leigh approached the little boy and knelt down in front of him. "Hi, Greggie," she said softly, taking his hand. "Want to play?"

The little boy bit down hard on three of her fingers. "Ow!" Leigh yelled, pulling her hand away and jumping to her feet. "He bit me! The little—." She stopped short when she saw Mrs. Webster hurrying toward her. Tears suddenly glistened in Leigh's eyes. "He bit me," she repeated when Mrs. Webster arrived. Leigh showed her the purplish-red teeth marks and specks of blood on her fingers.

"We've had a little problem with that," Mrs. Webster said. "I think he's just afraid. You'd better go wash that off. It looks like he broke the skin."

Leigh was happy for the chance to leave the little boy and retreat to the far corner of the room where the sink was.

Why didn't Jan tell me? Leigh thought as she let the cold water run over her hand. *First my pants and now this.*

Little Greggie hadn't moved from his spot when Leigh finished at the sink. But Leigh did notice that snot was not the only thing running down Greggie's face. Big tears welled from his eyes and spilled onto the little boy's shirt.

Leigh felt tears come to her own eyes as she

Shop 'Til You Drop

watched the little boy. He looked terrible. But worse yet, he looked so sad. Leigh couldn't take it anymore.

"Hi, Greggie," Leigh said for the second time. "Do you want to hear a story? A story about a little boy named Greggie?"

Two hours and about 50 books later, Leigh stopped rocking Greggie and put him back on the carpet.

"Time to go," Jan announced, appearing from out of nowhere. "How'd it go?"

"Great!" Leigh said with enthusiasm. "Greggie is the greatest. Aren't you, Greggie?"

Greggie grabbed Leigh's ankle and rubbed his face against her leg.

Mrs. Webster joined the little group. "Looks like you've made a friend already. Good work!"

Leigh pried the little fingers off of her ankle. "I'll see you tomorrow, Greggie. I promise."

Stepping out into the slightly chilly fall air, Leigh began her plans.

"Let's see. Friday is payday. After I pay Mom back her part, I should just have enough. Jan, could you do me a favor?"

"I will not!" Jan said firmly.

"You don't even know what I'm going to ask," Leigh argued, slightly offended.

"You may not borrow any money from me and that's final! You're in debt, remember?"

"I don't want your money," Leigh said with a laugh.

And Then God Made Laughter

Jan looked at Leigh suspiciously. "You don't?"

"I want you to go shopping for me. I'm grounded from the mall, remember?"

"Aha!" Jan cried. "I knew it!"

Leigh dropped her change into the bus's canister and found two seats near the back.

"It's not for me," Leigh continued. "It's for Greggie."

"Greggie?" Jan asked. "Now that's a change."

"I'll pay cash," Leigh said, counting on her friend's overly soft heart.

"OK! OK!" Jan laughed. "I'll do it. But shopping won't be the same without you."

"I don't mind," Leigh said slowly. "I'll have more time to spend with Greggie and the others. Spending time—now that's a new one."

"Yeah," Jan giggled. "And it's free!"

Leigh's prayer: Dear God, you sure do work in some weird ways. Whoever thought it would be more fun to spend time than money? And you know what I've figured out? It's not the "having" that's fun. It's the "getting." And today I just got something that I never could have found in a store. Thanks, God. Amen.

Action idea: Spend some time with somebody.

> "I can do everything through him
> who gives me strength."
> —Philippians 4:13

•

> *"Why, Barry, better watch it.
> I think you're about to say
> something positive."*
> —*Shauna*

The Building with Broken Windows

1

"You mean that old building off Nokomis Street?" Barry asked. "The one with all the broken windows and stuff?"

"Exactly!" Miss O'Hara, the eighth grade advisor, explained. "We'll be only three blocks from the playing field where the parade route is scheduled to begin. It's perfect."

As the rest of the students at the meeting began to discuss Miss O'Hara's attempt to find a suitable place for building the eighth grade homecoming float, Barry caught Shauna's attention from across the room. He pointed to his watch and then to the door, and Shauna signaled OK with her fingers. It had been a week since the high school student council had "graciously" offered to allow the seventh and eighth grade classes a chance to participate in this year's homecoming parade—grand prize $150! The parade was scheduled for two weeks from Saturday night. Shauna, Barry, and the rest of the eighth-grade student council representatives had scurried all week, securing supplies and finances from local businesses. Now that Miss O'Hara had found a place to work, they were ready to roll.

"So, what do you think?" Barry asked, catching Shauna at the end of the meeting.

"What do you mean what do I think?" Shauna asked. "Like Miss O'Hara said, 'It's perfect!' "

"Perfectly stupid, you mean," Barry continued. "No one seems to realize that these things can get vicious. I mean, there's money at stake here—"

"Not to mention class pride!" Shauna cut in, aware, as always, of her position as head cheerleader and class vice-president. "But what's your problem? We build a float—the best float—we win!" She started to walk away and Barry followed.

"But what about—," Barry stopped and looked up and down the now empty hallway. "Vandals!" he whispered. "If another class finds out where we're hiding it, we could lose it all. It's happened," he stated matter-of-factly. "Nokomis is just too close to school. We should build it in a nice, deserted barn about five miles out of town!"

"Oh, come on, Barry," Shauna said, stopping abruptly. "Don't be absurd. Who would want to vandalize a homecoming float? This is supposed to be

The Building with Broken Windows

fun, remember? Now go home and try to think of something more positive. Like a winning theme!" Shauna trotted down the hall.

"Don't say I didn't warn you," Barry called after the retreating Shauna. Shaking his head, he muttered to himself, "Nokomis Street—broken windows—anyone could get in if they wanted to. *Anyone!*"

A sudden dash of running feet echoed down the side corridor leading to the alley exit. Barry spun and ran to the corridor and looked down it in time to glimpse two pairs of skinny legs and one ponytail rush out. Had they heard? Was the eighth grade float already in jeopardy?

Don't be absurd, Barry remembered Shauna saying. He threw his jacket over his shoulder and headed for the exit. *Probably just a couple of seventh grade girls with a crush on you*, he tried to convince himself. Girls were always following Barry around or calling on the phone and then hanging up.

"Harmless," he muttered, trying to shrug off an uneasy feeling growing in the pit of his stomach. "Harmless—or is it?"

Barry's prayer: *God, maybe I'm worried about nothing, but some people's fun can be other people's worry. $150 can make people do some awfully strange things! Talk to you later, God. Barry.*

And Then God Made Laughter

The Building with Broken Windows

2

"Hey! We could have this giant football helmet with Wilson Warriors written on it and this huge shoe crushing it or something and...."

"Leave it to Ryan to come up with something violent!" Shauna whispered to Barry as they sat with the rest of the work crew on the old hay wagon that would, hopefully, become their winning float. "We've got to think more positively, more...."

Barry chuckled as Shauna jumped up and began her pep talk. *Leave it to Shauna to get things moving.*

"All right, you guys," Shauna began in her most authoritative voice. "What does our team have that Wilson doesn't? Come on. Think!" she coaxed.

"Cute guys!" Courtney shouted.

"Well, OK," Shauna encouraged. "But we just can't put cute guys all over the float."

"Why not?" Courtney asked. "The girls would vote for us."

"Get real, Courtney!" Ryan jumped in.

"And I suppose you think your crushed helmet was any better?" Courtney defended herself.

"Hey, you guys," Shauna said, moving the conversation away from Ryan and Courtney, "no idea is bad. Come on! Let's think! We can do it!"

Shauna's words echoed off the walls of the empty building. "We can do it, can do it, can do it."

"That's it!" Barry jumped up and joined Shauna. Shauna and the rest of the crowd looked at him blankly as Barry tried to regain his usual nonchalant composure. "I mean, you know," he continued, "like a slogan, a chant. Can do, can do," Barry repeated the words, trying to give the rest of the group the idea.

For a moment Barry stood before the staring, blank faces and felt his face turn red. "Uh, well, it was just an—idea," he said, forcing a laugh as he started to slink back to where he had sat.

"No, wait, Barry," Miss O'Hara said from the back of the group. "I like it! It's got a beat. Can't you hear it? Can do! Can do!" she repeated over and over until some of the kids started to catch on.

"Can do! Can do!" Shauna shouted, motioning to the others to join.

Soon the old building shook with the pounding of feet and the shouting of Barry's brainstorm.

"Can do! Can do! Can do!"

"Hey, we can still use my crushed helmet idea," Ryan tried once again.

"And a few cute guys won't hurt," Courtney added.

"How about the eighth grade cheerleaders on the float?" another voice added.

Soon the ideas were flying and in a week's time the old hay wagon started to take on a winning look. Chicken wire stretched across the back of the float with green and white crepe paper strung through so the words *Can Do* could be seen from blocks away. Instead of a crushed football helmet, a large goalpost wavered in the middle of the float, supported

The Building with Broken Windows

by two life-sized football players made from paper-mache and dressed in authentic uniforms begged from the football coach. Somebody had donated a piece of green outdoor carpet for the floor's turf and Ryan and a few others had pounded a large cardboard box into the slightly dented shape of a football.

Stepping back, the crew surveyed their work.

"Not bad," Barry decided. "A few finishing touches and—"

"Why, Barry," Shauna joked, "better watch it. I think you're about to say something positive."

"Hey! Somebody's got to be the realist around here," Barry retorted.

Shauna took another look at their week-long efforts. "Add the cheerleaders down in front and a couple of you guys in the back and—"

"How come the guys get the back of the float?" Ryan complained as he took one final whack at the cardboard football.

"Well, it doesn't matter, girls or guys, we just need a lot of volume to rev up the crowd," Shauna continued.

"We all worked. I say we all ride," somebody suggested from in back of the float.

"Fine with me. Any objections?" Shauna paused as she looked around the room. "OK! See you all back here Thursday after school. Only two days before we open the doors and show it to the world!"

"Speaking of doors," Barry said, suddenly serious, "did anyone notice the side entrance was open when we got here today?"

And Then God Made Laughter

"Probably Miss O'Hara forgot to lock up," someone suggested.

"Well, I'll check things over tonight," Barry volunteered, feeling suddenly suspicious. "I'd hate to see anybody try anything funny now."

"Those seventh graders wouldn't dare even look in the windows," Ryan snickered, punching the air with a one and a two.

Barry snorted, "What windows? Miss O'Hara didn't exactly pick the most secure place in town, you know."

"Never mind, Barry," Shauna sighed as the group filed out. "Anyone ever tell you you worry too much?"

"All the time," Barry countered. "All the time. That's why I'll take the keys, thank you."

"Suit yourself," Shauna said, tossing him the ring of keys as she flicked the light switch, leaving the float in the darkened room.

The Building with Broken Windows

3

"Will you please try to lighten up, Barry," Shauna complained as the group forged on ahead of them.

"I'm just telling you what I heard," Barry stated again.

"Well, I say just forget it," Shauna said with disgust. "Those seventh graders are always bragging about something. They're just trying to act big."

"No, really, Shauna. They didn't even know I could hear them. I was on the other side of the lockers," Barry answered in a worried whisper.

Shauna stopped at the corner to wait for the traffic. "So what did they say, again?" she asked, her mind more on catching up with the others than on Barry's rehash of some dumb seventh graders' conversation.

"Well, I didn't hear everything. . . ."

"Uh-huh?" Shauna said, trying to pay attention to Barry and get across the street at the same time.

"But I did hear the words *Nokomis Street, parade* and something about 'never having a chance now,' " Barry continued, unaware that Shauna was slowly losing patience. "I'm sure I locked up, but those seventh graders are really weasels. I mean, they'd do—"

Shauna suddenly stopped and turned toward Barry. "Not every seventh grader is out to get our float! Some of my best friends are seventh graders. Your problem, Barry, is that you're just a worry wart. You don't trust anyone, not even your friends! Take your

And Then God Made Laughter

time getting to the float. I'm sure you'll be disappointed if nobody has bothered to mess it up during the night."

Shauna huffed off, leaving Barry with his mouth hanging open and with nothing to say. Shauna never got mad. At least not that he had ever seen.

Barry slowly walked toward Nokomis Street. *It's not my fault Miss O'Hara picked such a stupid place to build the float. And I know that seventh grade class. They're up to something. I just don't know what.*

A block away from their building, Barry could hear Ryan yelling. "I'll rip their heads off, the little—jerks! Come on, guys. We're gonna find them!" Ryan called as he burst out the side door just as Barry rounded the corner.

Barry found himself surrounded by Ryan and the rest of the group, all demanding an explanation.

"Way to go, Bozo. Thought you said you'd lock up?" Ryan gave Barry's chest a push. "Well, it's trashed and I hope you're happy!"

"What's trashed? And I did lock up," Barry balked, trying to make sense out of everyone's accusations.

"Well, you must have forgotten something," Ryan said, cooling off a bit. "Come and look for yourself!"

Barry stared at him. "Oh, no," he moaned as he rushed into the old warehouse with the group following. Where the eighth grade float had once stood proudly, now only a few bits of green and white crepe paper hung from the support wire. Both of the football figures had been smashed beyond repair. The

The Building with Broken Windows

giant football and goalpost both had been kicked apart by the vandals.

Barry stood surveying the damage. "I knew it," he shook his head. "Those little jerks. I just knew it. It's trashed. Forget the parade. We're out."

"Are you sure you locked up?" Shauna asked, putting her hand on Barry's shoulder in a sort of apology.

"I locked up, I said!" Barry exploded, pushing her hand away. Then, more calmly, "When I say I'll lock up, I lock up. But there's more than one way to get into this building. Come on. Let's look around."

"Over here," Courtney called from behind some storage barrels. "I think I found the answer!"

"Those jerks!" Ryan yelled as he saw where someone had kicked in the wooden frame around one of the dilapidated windows. It was big enough for someone to crawl through without getting cut by the broken glass.

"Sorry, Barry," Shauna said loudly enough for the rest to hear. "I think we all owe Barry an apology."

"Yeah, sorry, man," Ryan said, slugging Barry's right arm. "I mean, we just all worked so hard, you know? Hard to see it all wasted. Come on, guys, we might as well start cleaning up."

Barry watched his friends walk back to the wagon and begin to tear down what was still pretending to be a float.

"Hey, wait! Wait, you guys. I just got an idea!"

And Then God Made Laughter

Barry surprised himself as he dashed toward the float and the rest of the group.

"Yeah, I got a few ideas, too," Ryan tried to joke as he jabbed at a stubborn piece of cardboard. "A few ideas about what to do to some little seventh graders!"

"No, I mean the float," Barry jumped up on the wagon. "The theme. You know—Can do! Well, can we or can't we? I say we can!"

"Can we or can't we what?" someone asked.

"Why can't we still finish our float before Saturday's parade?" Barry challenged, his fists clenched.

Courtney and a few others stopped sweeping debris from the wagon's floor.

"Come on, Barry. The parade's in two days. Get real. We'd never make it," Courtney said as several others nodded their heads.

"Never?" Barry asked, turning to the rest of the group. "Did I hear *never*? I say we can! Whoever did this thinks they got us. I say we prove them wrong!"

"How?" Ryan demanded. "We'd never—"

"Never?" Barry repeated a little louder with a grin on his face. "Did I hear the word *never*?"

Shauna and some others laughed.

"OK, Barry. Give us your plan," Shauna said, winking at the girls close to her. "I've never heard you so fired up!"

"OK," Barry took a deep breath. "Look. What really makes a float? People, right? Well, we've got

The Building with Broken Windows

people. Lots of people. Forget the goalpost and the football. We've still got the uniforms and time to redo the back and fix the floor. We'll fill the float with people. Fired-up people. Can-do people. A mob of people. A—"

"But not a word to anyone about what's happened," Shauna said in a loud whisper. "We'll just show up—"

"And take first place!" Courtney clapped.

"Can do?" Shauna asked those closest to her.

"Can do?" Barry asked, already digging in with the cleanup.

"Let's do it!" Ryan yelled, jumping up on the wagon.

"That's my man," Barry said, slapping him on the back. "Hey, Courtney! You got your wish! You're going to get your cute guys after all," he said, pointing to Ryan and himself.

"You two?" Courtney laughed. "Now we'll never win!"

"Never?" Barry scolded. "Did I—"

"Oh, can it!" Courtney said, throwing a piece of the cardboard football at them.

"Hey!" Barry jabbed Ryan. "I think we're being insulted."

"Can it! Can it!" Ryan and Barry chanted as they threw out garbage from under the wagon.

Ryan spoke up, "You know, we could still have this giant helmet being crushed, forget the giant shoe, but. . . ."

A few groaned and kept on working.

And Then God Made Laughter

"Is everyone having fun?" Barry yelled as the last of the plaster of paris left the wagon and hit the floor.

"Let's roll," Shauna yelled as once again they started to nail, glue, poke, and plan for the parade just two days away.

Barry's prayer: *Dear God, even with the worst thing happening we managed to pull it off—second place. All right!—and amen!*

Action idea: Are you a part of a team or special group? Next time you plan a project try a little "can do" and see what happens.

> "As you know, we consider blessed those who have persevered."
> —James 5:11

•

> *"Not you too, Janet. I'm beginning to feel like the Lone Ranger."*
> —Nancy

One Bottle of Pop on the Wall

1

"And what's so great about throwing up?" Nancy demanded of her best friend, Shari.

Shari just kept grabbing books and other stuff from her locker as she tried to beat the last bell before first hour.

"That's what usually happens, isn't it?" Nancy kept on. For once, she wasn't going to let Shari's silent treatment keep her from saying what needed to be said.

Taking a deep breath, Nancy continued. "So someone steals beer from their parents or somebody drinks too much and gets sick. Doesn't sound like fun to me. I thought parties were supposed to be fun."

And Then God Made Laughter

Nancy could tell Shari was listening even if she pretended not to. Shari always had this habit of snapping her gum whenever she was really nervous or really mad. Nancy watched as Shari gave one final snap and turned to face her friend.

"Well, I guess you won't know since you never come," Shari said, taking her gum from her mouth and sticking it on Nancy's locker as she slid past and headed down the hall.

Nancy could only watch Shari's retreating figure as her best friend walked off on her for the third time that week.

Trying not to lose face in front of the other kids still standing around the lockers, Nancy muttered, "Next time I want to vomit I'll be sure to be there!"

"Never mind her," Tina whispered with a knowledgeable look on her face. "She's just embarrassed you found out she was at Lonnie's party. Now that you know, she has to act like *you're* the weird one."

Nancy smiled slightly. Leave it to Tina to analyze Shari's rude behavior. Tina wanted to be a psychologist. She was always watching people at the mall or at basketball games and making comments on their behavior. Sometimes it got on Nancy's nerves, but today Tina's words almost seemed to make sense. How else could Nancy explain the change in her friend lately?

Nancy sighed. Life used to be so simple when *party* meant presents, games, and candles on your cake.

One Bottle of Pop on the Wall

"Almost seems like an epidemic, doesn't it?" Nancy continued later as she met Tina and a few others at their usual spot for lunch. "Seems everyone is partying. I hate it."

"Most of them are just lying," Janet's nasal voice cut in a little too quickly. "Take Melanie Meyers. You know how she bragged how sick she got at that party behind the old football field a few weeks ago? Well, Tom said she wasn't even there! Isn't she stupid?"

"Hmmm," Tina mused. "But how do you know Tom wasn't lying. Maybe he just wanted to prove he was there, too."

"Well, I don't—I hadn't—," Janet stammered. "Well, you know Melanie. She's always trying to act so cool about everything."

"Well, you can't believe everything you hear," Nancy said. "Let's talk about something else for a change."

"Shari was there, too," Janet continued, looking at Nancy.

Nancy felt like someone had punched her in the stomach. "So," she replied, giving Janet a look that could kill. "It's a free country! How do you know she was there?"

"Lonnie said she was pretty smashed," Janet smirked, quite aware that she now held the attention of the entire table.

"Since when are you on speaking terms with Lonnie?" Tina probed. Janet's eyes opened wide as she realized where Tina was taking the conversation.

And Then God Made Laughter

Tina watched Janet's face change from a smile to a scowl.

"I guess Shari wasn't the only one at that party—or at Lonnie's," Tina continued. "What was it you said about some people lying?"

Nancy and the others put down their lunches and looked at Janet.

"Not you, too, Janet?" Nancy almost moaned. "I'm beginning to feel like the Lone Ranger or something."

Janet's eyelids fluttered, but she soon recovered her composure, "Well, it's a free country. Can't a person have fun any way they want? Anyway, I was getting ready to invite you guys. I just wanted to see what you'd say."

"Right," Tina responded, not at all convinced.

Janet's mouth became pinched and tight as she fairly spit out her next words. "If you guys don't understand it, I can't explain it to you. You just have to be there. Don't you just like to get crazy once in a while?" Janet shot back, eyeing the table of girls. "Or are you all just a bunch of—"

"Go on," Tina commented, enjoying Janet's predicament.

"Oh, forget it!" Janet said, leaving her half-eaten lunch on the table as she stormed off.

Nancy sat motionless for a few seconds. "That's two today," she finally said to her remaining friends. "First Shari and now Janet. Who *didn't* go to Lonnie's party Friday night?"

"I didn't," Tina said matter-of-factly.

One Bottle of Pop on the Wall

"Who needs it," another girl smirked. "Did you see Lonnie's face today? He looks sick!"

"That's the whole purpose of partying," Tina explained. "Party 'til you puke, right?"

"Where did you hear that one?" Nancy almost smiled.

"Gross!" another girl groaned.

"It's true," Tina laughed. "I saw it written on Janet's science notebook. On the inside cover, of course!"

"I can't believe Shari and Janet would become partiers," Nancy shook her head. "If *they're* drinking, who's next?"

Nancy's prayer: Lord, I don't want to be a Lone Ranger. I just want to be myself. Does that mean I'm weird? Help me to understand Shari. Janet I can do without! Amen.

And Then God Made Laughter

2

"Behind the old football field."

"Friday night. After the game."

"Make something up. Tell them you're sleeping over at my house. My parents are gone for the weekend."

"What do you mean you don't know? Come on, everyone is going."

Nancy could only hear one side of the conversation as she pretended to be looking for a specific book in a back corner of the library. She didn't have to see who was on the other side of the stacks. Anyone could recognize Janet's nasal voice.

Someone should tell her parents to have her adenoids removed, Nancy thought as she pulled a reference book from the bottom shelf. And then she heard it. *Snap.* Gum. Shari's gum.

"I don't know, Janet," Shari had turned so her voice was now distinguishable.

Nancy pulled a book off the shelf and peered into the next aisle.

Shari took her gum out of her mouth and stuck it on the end of the book shelf she was leaning on. Nancy thought she still looked nervous even if she wasn't snapping her gum.

"I don't know," Shari repeated. "Did you really have fun at Lonnie's party? I thought it was kind of stu—"

"Fun?" Janet exploded. "It was a blast. I've never

One Bottle of Pop on the Wall

been so smashed. Come on, you liked it, didn't you?"

"Well, yeah, I guess I did after all," Shari said slowly.

"Of course you did. I just know you had a blast," Janet remarked in her nasal voice. "We all did."

Shari tried to sound enthusiastic, "Yeah, I guess it was a blast."

"OK, well, be there Friday," Janet said as she gathered her books. "Lonnie will be looking for you."

Lonnie! Nancy mouthed silently. *As if Shari would even look twice at that creep.*

"I'll call you tonight, OK?" Janet whispered as one of the library aides walked past their aisle.

From behind the oversized reference books, Shari didn't appear as confident as she had yesterday by Nancy's locker. Nancy waited until Janet had left. "Pssst! Shari!" Nancy called between the empty spaces of the books into the next aisle.

"Agh!" Shari yelped, jumping about two feet in the air.

"It's me! Nancy!"

"Where are you?" Shari snapped as she began grabbing books off the shelf, trying to find Nancy. Finally their eyes met.

"What are you doing?" Shari demanded.

"I was just about to ask you the same thing," Nancy said, taking another book from the shelf so she could see Shari's face. "You're not really going to go, are you? Janet's a jerk. And Lonnie! You always said he had the worst body odor in the school!" Nancy stopped and then began again, "And besides, I miss you. You don't need it, Shari. It's stupid; you said it yourself."

Shari's eyes flashed suddenly. "I did not," she snapped.

"Well, you were going to," Nancy said in a more quiet voice.

Shari looked away from Nancy's intense gaze and said nothing. For a moment Nancy thought she was in for another of Shari's silent treatments.

Suddenly, Shari leaned closer, sticking her face into the place where an outdated version of *The Origin of Man* should have been.

"You just don't understand, Nanc," Shari whispered, with a look on her face that even Tina would have had a hard time analyzing. "You just don't understand."

"Then tell me," Nancy pleaded. "I'm your friend. I'm—"

But Shari's face had disappeared behind the books and by the time Nancy reached the next aisle only Shari's gum, still hanging on the dusty bookrack, remained.

Shari's prayer: Dear God, I know you created me for something better than a beer party. Help me find my way back to you and the people who really like me for who I am, not for what I do. Amen.

One Bottle of Pop on the Wall

3

"It's the only way," Tina whispered nervously as she groped her way through the crowd of kids already gathered behind the old football field.

Nancy pulled her hat down lower over her eyes and kept her head down. "This is embarrassing. What if someone recognizes us?" she whispered.

"Just be quiet and keep looking. She's got to be here somewhere," Tina whispered back. "What about over there where the cliff starts to go up?"

"There's lots of people here. But no one from our school. They look a lot older," Nancy commented, lifting her head for a minute.

A boy with pimples and curly hair started to move towards them, looking a little too friendly. He had a beer in each hand.

"Quick! We've been spotted!" Nancy gasped as she grabbed Tina's arm and dragged her toward some nearby bushes.

The pimply faced boy walked past the two girls as if they didn't even exist.

"Will you relax!" Tina said, shaking herself lose from Nancy's grasp. "We're here for one reason and one reason only. To get Shari and leave. That's it. Now start looking!"

A loud, nasal giggle came from behind the scraggly trees on the left.

Janet! both Tina and Nancy mouthed to each other silently.

And Then God Made Laughter

Sneaking around away from the largest part of the crowd, Tina and Nancy crept cautiously past the brush and peered between two dead branches of a tree.

"There she is!" Tina said, pointing toward a small group of kids gathered by a campfire.

"Is that Lonnie who's got his arm around her? Yuck! How can she stand it?" Nancy paused. "What should we do now? We found her. What if she doesn't want to go?"

"I'll think of something. But look at her face. Doesn't look like she's having too good a time." Tina peered a little closer into the glow of the fire.

Nancy had already noticed the look on Shari's face as well as the steady snap, snap, snap of her gum. She'd only seen that look on Shari's face once before and that was when her cat had died. It didn't make sense. If she didn't want to be here, then why did she come?

"Shhh!" Tina suddenly signaled. "Listen!"

"Anyone thirsty?" Lonnie asked as he leaped up and headed toward the group of older kids gathered around the metal barrel. "My brother's on duty tonight. I'm sure I can get something from him."

Janet laughed and tossed her hair over her shoulder. "Don't drink any on the way back!" she yelled, trying her hardest to look nonchalant.

"Hey, Shari!" Lonnie yelled back, holding up one finger.

Shari looked increasingly more uncomfortable. "Ah—I—," she stumbled for words.

One Bottle of Pop on the Wall

"Ah, get her two," Janet said. "Loosen up, Shari. You act as if your mother's watching or something." Shari stared at the fire. Janet looked at her sideways, "Feeling bad about what you told your parents? Come on, they'll never know. That is, unless you tell. I'm going to see what's keeping Lonnie."

Janet moved out of the light from the fire and away from Tina's and Nancy's hiding place.

"Now's our chance!" Tina said, moving closer to Shari, who looked like she was about to cry.

"Grab her!" Nancy said, nudging Tina forward faster than she had planned.

Tina turned and glared at the startled Nancy. "Will you pleeease relax!" Tina said, shaking Nancy's hand off her arm one more time. "I'm just going to talk to her, OK?"

Moments later a startled Shari looked up into the faces of her two friends.

"Eek!" Shari half screamed, looking back and forth between Tina and what she thought was Nancy under the hat. "What are you doing here?" she finally asked, gasping for air. "You scared me!"

"Never mind," Tina said. "We can talk about that later. Right now, there's a group of kids down at Jake's pizza having a great time. We just came to see if you wanted to come."

Shari looked as if she was going to laugh, cry, and hug her friends all at the same time. "Yeah," she gasped, "I'd love to come."

Tina and Nancy looked at each other with relief.

And Then God Made Laughter

"Hey, Tina! Is that you, Nancy? Way to be cool, man!"

It was Janet.

"Sorry, we were just leaving," Tina teased slightly.

"Yeah, we're outta here," Nancy said, following Tina.

"I should have guessed," Janet sneered. "Too much for you youngsters to handle, huh?" she laughed, looking at Shari for support.

Janet's sneer turned into a gasp as Shari stood up and began to follow her friends. "Thanks anyway, Janet. I won't be needing a place to stay tonight. We're going for pizza. Want to come?"

Janet just stood there staring at the retreating figures. "You guys—," she whined.

In the dark, Tina, Nancy, and Shari grabbed hands and then hugged.

"Thanks," Shari whispered as they left the party and headed downtown.

"Hey, what are friends for?" Tina smiled.

Nancy just gave her friend another hug. "Come on, you guys. Hurry up. I'm starving!"

"One large pepperoni and sausage pizza coming up!" Shari said with a big smile. "And a large pitcher of pop!"

Nancy's prayer: *We had a great time tonight, Lord, once we got to Jake's. I still don't understand what's so great about partying. But then, who needs to, right? Amen.*

One Bottle of Pop on the Wall

Action idea: Why do you think kids party? Write down 10 ways to have fun without drinking and then go and do all of them!

And Then God Made Laughter

"And the Lord's servant must not quarrel;
instead, he must be kind to everyone,
able to teach, not resentful."
—2 Timothy 2:24

•

"Let it be a game, Karla. Have fun!"
—Coach Buckley

The Killer Instinct

1

Karla swung hard at the volleyball. *Whack!* A perfect spike and her school's team regained the serve. "Way to go, Karla!" Coach Buckley yelled from the sideline.

Karla didn't take time to acknowledge her words. "Come on! Fire up!" Karla shouted at her teammates.

Cindy, the tallest girl on the school volleyball team and also Karla's best friend, landed her new jump serve deep near the back line.

"They're setting it up," Karla screamed at the front row. "Watch it! Watch it! Move, move, move!"

Almost in slow motion, the other team maneuvered the ball to the front line. The short red-haired girl jumped as if to take the final hit—

And Then God Made Laughter

"Watch it!" Karla screamed louder. "It's a—"

The ball, driven by another team member who had moved in suddenly for the kill, slammed down hard upon the front line and bounced off into the bleachers.

"Fake," Karla finished her sentence after the fact.

Karla stood with her hands on her hips for a few seconds and then kicked her toe hard into the floor. "Get with it," Karla yelled. "If you don't want to win, don't play!"

One of the girls in the front line who had just missed getting the dig turned and shouted, "I suppose you could've done better, Hot Stuff. You're not the coach, Karla, so quit acting like it."

Karla just tossed her teammates a "so what" look and turned to throw the ball back to the other side.

The ball came back—an overhand serve to Cindy whose return sent it out of bounds. The other team screamed in excitement. Game over.

"Great," Karla muttered, stalking off the court and into the dressing room. "What a bunch of losers. Wish I was on a team that cared about winning for once."

Karla showered ahead of the others and finished dressing as the rest of the team entered the locker room. Hidden behind the back lockers, Karla could hear their conversation, but she remained hidden from their sight.

"Looks like Miss Hot Stuff's gone home already. What a baby."

The Killer Instinct

"Did you hear her get down on Amy when she hit that ball that would have gone out?"

"On Amy? What about all of us? 'Move, move, move!'" The other girls laughed as someone mimicked Karla's on-court cheerleading.

"All she ever thinks about is winning."

Coach Buckley yelled into the locker room. "Nice effort, girls! We'll get them next time. Showers!"

Karla waited until she could hear the rest of the team laughing and joking in the shower room before coming out of her hiding place.

So that's what they think of me. I'm the only one who really cares about winning! They just want to have fun. Well, I can't have fun if I don't win!

Karla threw her stuff into her gym bag and banged open the door to the hallway.

"Hey! Take it easy," Coach Buckley said, jumping out of the way. "Good game, Karla!"

"We lost," Karla mumbled and kept on walking.

Coach Buckley was not easily put aside. Catching up to Karla, she put a hand on Karla's shoulder. "What's going on, Karla?" the coach asked. "It's not like you to act this way."

Karla stopped, put her gym bag down and looked her coach in the eye. "I hate losing. Nobody cares if we win or lose but me. And now everybody hates me because of it. I wish they'd grow up or quit."

Coach Buckley spied an open classroom. "Let's talk in there. I have something that might surprise you."

And Then God Made Laughter

Karla's prayer: *Dear God, is it so wrong to want to win? I'm sorry I get so mad at everybody but I can't help it.*

The Killer Instinct

2

"I like your style, Karla," Coach Buckley began. "You're a real go-getter. You're assertive. You work hard. You expect the best from yourself and from your teammates."

Karla's shoulders slumped. "They don't care if we win or lose. It's all a game to them."

"But that's all it is, Karla," Coach Buckley said softly. "A game. There's nothing wrong with wanting to win. Don't get me wrong. But what really matters is that you enjoy playing the game."

Karla stared at Coach Buckley. "I like to play. I like everything there is about volleyball. The serves, the slams—"

"And especially the scores!" Coach Buckley broke in with a chuckle. "I know. I used to be just like you."

Karla gulped, "You did?"

"You bet. And I must admit my teammates didn't like me either." Coach Buckley paused, remembering her playing days. "Yeah, I was good. No," the coach laughed, "I was great! But my team? Well. . . ."

"So, what did you do?" Karla asked with more than a little interest.

"Well," Coach Buckley replied, "I felt sorry for myself for a while. But then I decided I was only going to compete with myself. You know. Be as hard as I wanted to be on me. I would expect the most from Jeanne Buckley and leave the rest up to the others on the team."

"So what happened?" Karla urged, not quite sure what the coach was trying to say.

"It was contagious," Coach Buckley laughed. "When the others saw how hard I was trying, well, they started trying too."

Karla smiled, "And did you win?"

"Sometimes," Coach Buckley continued. "But even when the points said we lost, we still felt like winners, because we all did our best. We felt proud."

Coach Buckley smiled and stood up. "Lecture over. Think about it, OK?"

Karla felt that bitter feeling in her stomach start to melt. "Yeah," she said, slowly. "I'll do more than think."

"That's a winner, Karla!" Coach Buckley fairly beamed. "That's a winner!"

Karla's prayer: *Dear God, I still like to be the best, Lord. And that's good. Now help me learn to help others be their best, too. Amen.*

Action idea: Next time you play a game, see how many encouraging comments you can make to the other people on your team. You may not win, but you'll sure have fun trying.

> "And do not forget to do good and
> to share with others, for with
> such sacrifices God is pleased."
> —Hebrews 13:16

•

"Mom? Can we stop on the way at a florist?"
—*Lisa*

For Grandma

1

"Emily! Stop that!"

"Erick, get down. Erick!"

Too late. A half-full box of what was to be the morning snack fell from the kitchen counter while four chubby hands grabbed raisin after raisin from off the floor.

Lisa sighed and got out the broom for the third time that morning. "All right you two, that's it!" she said in her sternest voice. "One more spill and there's no Sesame Street!"

Emily and Erick stopped gobbling raisins. Sesame Street was their favorite show.

"Sor-ry, Lisee," Erick lisped as he jumped up and ran toward the TV room, leaving Emily to try and finish off the few remaining dust-covered morsels.

And Then God Made Laughter

"Me want Sesame Street, Lisee," Emily whimpered quietly. "Peese?"

Lisa stooped down to cradle the little girl. "OK, Emily, but no more raisins."

Emily wiggled free. "Yea—Sesame, Sesame, Sesame," she echoed, jumping up and down on the remaining raisins that had somehow escaped the little gobblers.

"Emily! Emi—stop! You're getting raisins on your shoes. Emi!" Lisa hollered.

But Emily was already halfway to the family room, leaving sticky patches of raisin embedded in the hall carpet.

Lisa faked a silent scream and began scraping raisin residue off the floor with her fingernails. *Only two more Saturdays and I'll have the last $20 payment for the dress*, she reminded herself.

Lisa had been working every Saturday morning for the last three months for her dentist, Dr. Evans, and his wife while they played tennis at a nearby center. Lisa knew if it weren't for the dress she had put on lay-away three months earlier, she would have given up this job long ago.

"I'm sorry, Lisa," her mom had said, glancing at the price tag on the dress. "I know it's your first dance and it is a beautiful dress. But this price is really out of line. I could redo the dress Audrey wore last year. No one at school would recognize it and you're almost the same size."

"But I want my own dress," Lisa had complained. "I always have to wear Audrey's old things."

For Grandma

Lisa's mother smiled one of her "I know" smiles, paused, and then said, "You know, Lisa, you could put it on lay-away and pay a little each month. There's time before the dance. But it is a big commitment and it takes a lot of responsibility to make those payments."

And so Lisa had signed away her next 12 Saturday mornings for payments on a dress.

Not just any dress, Lisa reminded herself as she listened for sounds of Cookie Monster and Big Bird from the family room down the hall.

"Me want cookie! Me love cookie!" Lisa heard Erick chant. Funny. Even at three Erick almost sounded like the real Cookie Monster.

"Me want cookie! Me love cookie!"

"My cookie, my cookie," Emily suddenly screamed back.

Lisa jumped up and headed for the family room to retrieve Emily's shoes and stop the quarrel.

"OK, you two—" Lisa stopped, horrified at the scene in front of her.

Up on tippy-toe, hands holding her "cookie" high above her head, Emily balanced on top of the TV console. "My cookie," she screamed, kicking at Erick with one of her sticky, brown shoes.

Erick chuckled mischievously. "Me want cookie, me want cookie," he growled in his best Cookie Monster voice.

Lisa lunged forward. "No Emily, get down! Careful! That's not a cookie, Emi. That's—"

89

And Then God Made Laughter

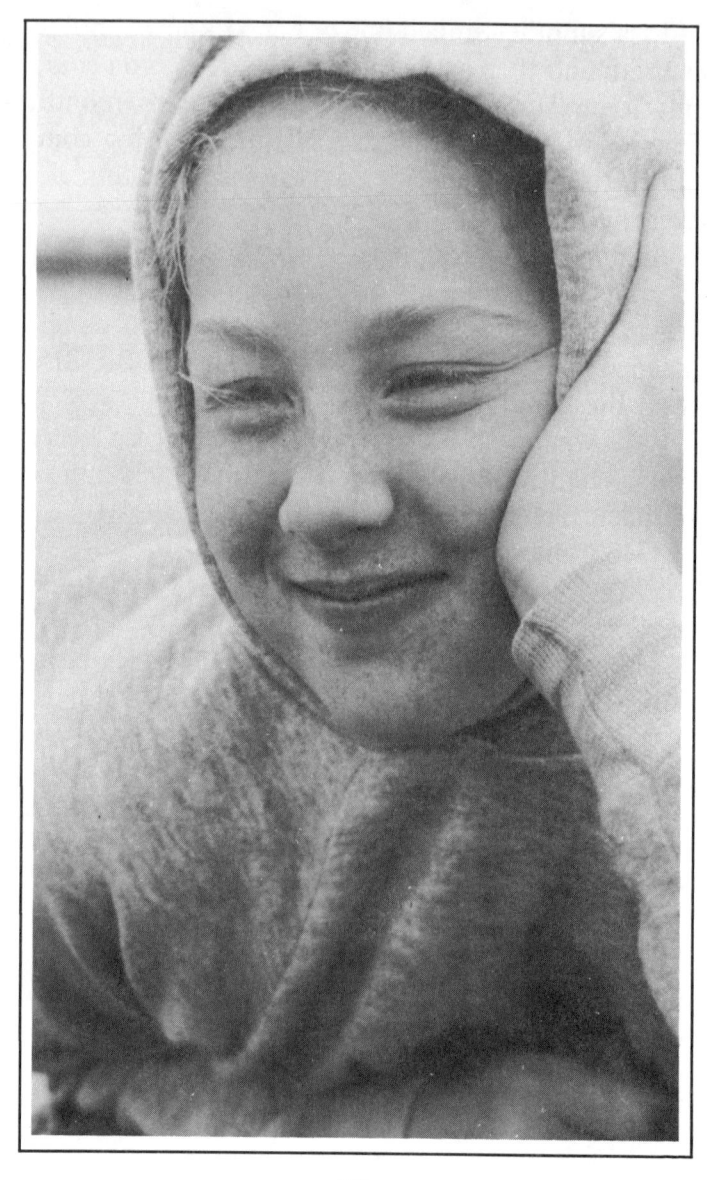

For Grandma

Crash.
Silence.
"Your mother's favorite dish," Lisa's voice trailed off.
"Sor-ry, Lisee."
"Two more weeks. Just two more weeks," Lisa lamented as she headed for the dustpan one more time.

Lisa's prayer: *Dear God, why does making money have to be so much work? I deserve that dress. I've earned it and I'm going to have it! Love, Lisa. Amen.*

And Then God Made Laughter

2

Lisa let the back door slam as she looked around the kitchen for some leftover lunch.

"Anyone home?" she yelled out, not really expecting an answer.

Audrey usually spent Saturday afternoons at the college library studying—or so she said. Lisa was pretty sure that good old Audrey was only at the library because she had a crush on the tall, good-looking guy who worked in the reference room. Audrey had never been one to study without a real reason, and when she did the reason usually had something to do with a guy.

Lisa poured a glass of milk, taking the glass with her into the garage. Blue car gone. Mom must be shopping. Maybe Gram went with her.

Lisa stole a glance into the backyard through the garage window. A gray head covered with a red bandana peeked out from behind some bushes.

Grandma Kelly had been living with Lisa and her family for two years now, ever since her dad's and mom's divorce. Lisa still wasn't used to the fact that her parents didn't live together anymore, but somehow having Grandma around helped fill the empty gap.

"Hi, Gram," Lisa yelled through the open window. "Survived another morning with Erick and Emily! What you doing?"

"Oh, just pulling a few weeds," Gram said, wiping

For Grandma

her forehead with the back of her hand. "But I think I've had enough. Time to sit down. Meet you back inside and you can tell me all about what your little friends cooked up today."

Later, as they sat at the kitchen table, Lisa laughed, "And then Emily tracked raisin all the way into the TV room."

Grandma laughed, too. "You've got your hands full, that's for sure. I remember when you and Audrey were about that age. We managed to pull you two apart now and then whenever you really got into it." Grandma smiled. "But you girls turned out pretty good, I'd say. Have another cookie?" Grandma asked, passing her special peanut butter cookies to Lisa.

"Me want cookie!" Lisa pretended to yell, remembering Erick's antics. "Well, anyway they paid me and I only have two more Saturdays left before I can pick up my dress, paid in full!"

"Oh yes, the dress," Grandma said, moving the lunch dishes over to the sink. "I'm really proud of how you've kept at that bill. Quite a hefty sum, your mother said."

"Just wait until you see it, Gram. I mean, when I put it on I really feel, well—"

"Beautiful?" Grandma prompted.

"Yeah," laughed Lisa, "or at least passable enough for someone to ask me to dance!"

"You'll probably have to fight them off," Grandma said with a wink. "Think I'll go upstairs and rest before your mom comes home."

And Then God Made Laughter

Lisa rinsed the dishes and began stacking them in the dishwasher. *Gram always has time for me*, she thought happily. *Someday I'm going to do something really nice for her, too.*

A loud thud rattled the cup in Lisa's hand. Even before she heard Grandma's moan she knew something serious had happened.

"Grandma!" Lisa yelled as she ran toward the living room.

Grandma lay at the foot of the steps, her face ghostly white against the red bandana still on her head.

"It's OK, Lisa," she whispered, "but you'd better call the ambulance. I think I've broken my hip."

Lisa's mother came home right when the ambulance pulled out of the drive with its flashing red lights.

"Lisa, what's happened? Is it Grandma? Is she all right?" her mother asked, dropping her packages on the counter.

"Yes, I think so." Lisa's hands were still shaking. "It's her hip. She tripped on the stairs and—"

"Those old throw rugs. Should have thrown them out long ago," Mrs. Snider said, wringing her hands together. "You stay here and wait for Audrey. I'll follow the ambulance."

"But Mother—"

"Wait!" Mrs. Snider said sharply.

Lisa bit her lip. Crying wasn't going to help anyone now.

Mrs. Snider paused and then gave Lisa a hug.

For Grandma

"I'm sorry, Lisa. It was scary, wasn't it, Honey? But you did a good job and I'm sure Gram will be just fine. I'll call you from the hospital when I get there."

Lisa watched the blue hatchback pull out of the driveway. "Please be OK, Grams. Please," she whispered, wiping away tears with the red bandana the ambulance attendant had handed her.

Lisa's prayer: *Dear God, Grandma needs you tonight, so I won't be long. What can I do to show her I really care? Love, Lisa. Amen.*

3

"Grandma needs her rest, Lisa. We'll go tomorrow," Mrs. Snider said, taking off her coat. "They're going to put a pin in her hip so she'll be in for more than a few days. She needs rest tonight. She's had quite a day."

"Audrey! Where have you been?" Lisa demanded as the back door opened and a breathless Audrey scurried in.

"Little sisters don't have to know everything!" Audrey teased, tossing her coat over the chair. "Hey, what's up?" Audrey paused, looking at the two worried faces staring at her. "Listen, if you're mad 'cause I'm late, I locked my keys in the car and this cute guy from the resource room helped me out—"

"It's not you, Audrey," Mrs. Snider said wearily. "It's Grandma. She had a fall and—"

Audrey's jaw dropped. "Grandma? Is she all right?"

"She's in the hospital," Lisa answered. "We can go see her tomorrow."

"Mom?" Audrey cast a questioning glance at Mrs. Snider.

"She'll be fine, Audrey. But I'm glad you girls are here. It helps to be together tonight."

The next day, after lunch, Lisa stood staring out her window with her hands on the knobs of her dresser drawer. She stood thoughtfully for a long time. Then, carefully, she took two $10 bills from

For Grandma

her top drawer, folded them into her wallet, and hurried downstairs.

"Come on, girls! Visiting hours start in 20 minutes!" Mrs. Snider yelled from the kitchen.

Lisa scrambled into her usual spot in the car and waited for Audrey to join them.

"Mom?" Lisa asked, leaning over the front seat. "Can we stop on the way at a florist? I want to get Grandma some flowers."

"No, Honey, you need to save your money for that dress. I'll order some from all of us later," Mrs. Snider said, trying to comb her hair in the small mirror of the car.

"No. I want this to be from me," Lisa said firmly.

Mrs. Snider put her comb down and turned around. "But Lisa, you need your money for your dress. The dance is only two weeks away. You haven't forgotten?"

Lisa paused only slightly. "I can wear Audrey's dress. It'll look OK. Really, Mom. I can have as much fun in her dress as the new one."

"You really mean that, don't you, Lisa," Mrs. Snider said. "Well, I'm proud of you. And yes, we can stop at Lund's on the corner across from the hospital."

"Let's go," Audrey said, finally jumping into the car.

"We'll be a little late anyway," Lisa explained. "Audrey, we're going to make a stop and, by the way, can I borrow that blue sweater dress you wore last year? There's this cute guy . . . ," Lisa mocked in her most flirtatious voice.

Audrey stared at her younger sister. "What's gotten into her?" she asked, looking at her mother for an answer.

Mrs. Snider laughed. "Just a little joy, Audrey, and a lot of growing up!"

"Sisters," Audrey muttered, shaking her head. "I'll never understand them!"

Lisa's prayer: Dear God, Grandma loved the flowers and she knew they were just from me, too. It was fun to bring her something special even though it meant giving up something I wanted. Sometimes giving can be almost as much fun as getting. But you already know that, don't you, God. Love, Lisa. Amen.

Action idea: Giving doesn't always have to mean money. You can give up an hour of sleep on a Saturday morning to do an extra few chores around the house. Or try giving up a night out with your friends and volunteer to babysit a younger brother or sister. Give up something. You'll be surprised what you get back in return.

"He has made everything beautiful in its time."
—Ecclesiastes 3:11

•

*"So it wasn't just a joke.
Carrie was telling the truth."*
—Samantha

Here's Looking at You

1

"Hey, look at this," Carrie said in a loud whisper, shoving a copy of *Seventeen* under Samantha's nose. "Can you believe that's the same person?"

Samantha glanced at the picture under Carrie's finger and then glanced at the librarian to see if he was watching.

"She looks—crooked," Samantha finally said. "I don't get it."

"Well, see," Carrie began, "They only photographed half her face."

Samantha still looked confused. "Well then, why am I looking at her whole face?" Samantha said, beginning to suspect this was another of Carrie's jokes. Carrie was always telling Sam stuff that sounded almost believable and as soon as Sam fell for it Carrie got her big laugh. It was getting tiresome.

And Then God Made Laughter

"Because they used the same photograph twice—only reversing it. See?" Carrie asked, holding her math notebook over half the photo. "It only looks funny when you put the same photo next to the other one."

Carrie paused to read some of the article. "It says that everyone's face has two sides; there's a dark side and a light side." Carrie held her notebook over half her face. "Notice anything?"

Samantha shook her head, not quite ready to take Carrie seriously.

"OK, what about now?" Carrie asked, switching the notebook to the other side of her face.

Sam saw it right away. "Hey, you're right. One side does look different from the other."

Carrie laughed. "It better, or we would look like that!" she said, pointing to the photograph in the magazine. Carrie tossed her notebook across the table. "Let's see you."

Samantha felt silly covering part of her face with a notebook scribbled with names of boys and girls, some crossed out, some with hearts around them. Somehow Carrie always had the scoop on who liked whom and who didn't like whom.

OK, *here it comes. The punch line. The big laugh*, Samantha thought to herself as Carrie continued to peer at her face.

"OK, now the other side," Carrie ordered. Samantha obediently moved the notebook from left to right.

If I could only think of a clever comeback, something

Here's Looking at You

to let Carrie know I knew this was a joke all along.
Samantha paused in her plans and looked at Carrie. Something was wrong.

"Move it back," Carrie said in a worried voice. "Now the other side again." There was a long silence as Carrie continued staring at first the right side and then the left side of Samantha's face.

"What's wrong," Samantha finally demanded.

Carrie took a deep breath. "They're the same," she said matter-of-factly.

"What's the same?" Samantha asked.

"Your face. There's no difference. You look—"

Samantha sat horrified. "Like that!" she shrieked, grabbing the magazine out of Carrie's hands.

Carrie's serious expression broke up as she started to laugh. "You are so gullible!" she panted, holding her side. "Really Sam, did you think your face—Sam? Hey, Sam, it was just a joke!"

But Sam had already passed the librarian's desk heading for any place that was out of the sight and hearing of Carrie Yetter.

Carrie's prayer: *Dear God, how was I to know Samantha would get so upset? It was just a joke, right? Well anyway, it made her feel bad. Help me find a way to make it up to her. Amen.*

And Then God Made Laughter

Here's Looking at You

2

"Hi, Sam!" her dad yelled as the screen door slammed, announcing Sam's arrival home.

"Hi, Dad!" Sam yelled back, trying to keep her voice steady so he wouldn't notice anything was wrong. "I'm going upstairs."

"The plumber is in the bathroom," Mr. Sabin yelled back. But Sam was already out of earshot.

Privacy! That's what I need! Sam mused as she threw her books on her bed and headed for the only room in the house with a lock on the door. Closing the bathroom door behind her, Samantha leaned back against the full-length mirror her mom had insisted on adding somewhere in the house. Alone at last.

"Be done in a minute," Mr. Reneck, the plumber, announced, sticking his head out from behind the shower curtain. "Got a bad drip here."

"Ahhhh!" screamed Sam in surprise. She yanked open the bathroom door and retreated to her own bedroom.

"The only drip in this house is me!" she announced to her mirror, which was shaking now from the good slamming she had given the bedroom door.

Samantha sat slumped against the side of her bed and watched the mirror settle back down against the blue-flowered wallpaper that had been on her walls since she was six.

Taking one of her notebooks from the pile on the

And Then God Made Laughter

bed, Sam marched over and confronted herself in the mirror. "Carrie and her stupid ideas," she muttered, covering first the left and then the right side of her face.

Sam moved closer to the mirror for an in-depth inspection. Stepping back, she snapped the notebook across to the other side. Left then right. Back to the left. She paused.

Well, they're not exactly the same, Sam thought, scowling that she had even begun this little experiment. *But my nose does seem a little bit. . . .* Sam stuck her face back up to the mirror. Her breath fogged up the reflection so she wiped it off with her hand and held her breath as she zeroed in on the center of her face. "Dad, where's the tape measure?" she yelled, fogging up the mirror again.

"Yardstick's in the garage!" Mr. Sabin yelled back.

"Yardstick? Good grief!" Sam laughed, getting up to find it herself. She opened the door and jolted to a stop. Mr. Reneck was standing in the hall, just ready to knock on her door, a tape measure in a shiny, silver case in his hand.

"Keep it! It's on the house. Good for advertising," he explained as he headed down the stairs.

Sam looked at the silver square in her hand with the words *Reneck Plumbing* in red letters printed across the front. *It's metal but it'll bend,* she decided as she headed for the bathroom, locking the door firmly behind her.

Let's see, Sam thought. *If I measure from the center*

Here's Looking at You

of my ear to the tip of my nose and then from the other side, that should do it!

"Four and three-quarter inches!" she announced aloud. Switching hands, Sam carefully held the end of the measure against her other ear and calculated the distance to her nose. "Four and—five-eighths?"

"It *is* crooked!" she whispered, checking her calculations for a third time. "Exactly one-eighth of an inch to the left."

Sam slumped down, devastated. So it wasn't just a joke. Carrie was telling the truth. *My face—it's crooked.* Sam pulled herself back up and scowled into the mirror. *So what. So my nose isn't exactly in the center of my face.*

Sam unwrinkled her forehead, paused, and then scowled again. She did it again and again, scowling and smiling at herself in the mirror. With exact calculations it appeared that if she scowled, her nose moved just a little to the right. Just a little. An eighth of an inch little. Right to the center of her face.

Sam stared at the scowling girl in the mirror. *It does look just a little crabby,* she thought, turning her head side-to-side. *Maybe if I scowled and smiled at the same time—you know, the serious but friendly look.* Sam scowled and then smiled. Her nose appeared to center itself perfectly.

It's all Carrie's fault, Sam argued silently, trying to keep her smile and her scowl in place. *I was perfectly happy with my face until this.* Sam sighed, unlocked the bathroom door, and headed downstairs for the real test.

And Then God Made Laughter

Sam's prayer: *Dear God, is everyone's nose in the center of their face? I wish I'd never started this whole mess! Amen.*

Here's Looking at You

3

Sam's dad was just pulling his head out from under the kitchen sink as Sam stuck her head in the refrigerator to see what there was to eat. "That takes care of all the drips in this house!" he announced in a well-satisfied voice. "How about a snack, Sam? I'm—" Mr. Sabin's voice stopped in mid-sentence as he stared at Sam with a half-puzzled, half-concerned look on his face.

Sam tried to act as natural as possible so as not to affect her dad's reaction too much. Sam could always trust her dad to tell her the truth. If she looked funny, her dad would tell her right up front. No jokes. Not on serious matters.

"Well?" Sam finally countered.

Mr. Sabin chuckled slightly as he pulled up a chair and looked straight into Sam's face. "I don't quite know what to say. Care to explain?"

"It's my nose. It's off center. I'm trying to fix it," Sam answered, screwing her eyebrows a little tighter together and increasing her smile just a touch.

Mr. Sabin's chuckle turned into a small cough as he peered at his daughter's nose. "And where did you get this idea that your nose is crooked?" he asked as he began to spread mustard across the top of the pastrami Sam had handed him.

"It's a long story," Sam sighed, remembering Carrie and that weird picture in the magazine that had started the whole thing. "Do you think it looks

OK?" Sam asked matter-of-factly. "I want your honest answer."

"You sure?" Mr. Sabin asked, taking a final look at the concerned Sam.

"For sure!" Sam promised.

"OK," Mr. Sabin said. "I think it looks funny."

"Dad!" Sam yelled, ruining any attempt to keep her nose in the middle of her face. "This is serious."

"I know, I know," Mr. Sabin mumbled through his pastrami. "And I told you the truth. I've always thought your nose was kind of cute. And even if it was crooked, so is everyone else's. Nobody's face is exactly perfect, you know. Look at mine," Mr. Sabin laughed, giving Sam his famous Mr. Ed impression.

"Dad!" Sam said again, this time with a little less energy.

"Well, it's true. If there's one thing your mom and I know how to make, it's pretty girls. See, now here's a pretty girl!" Mr. Sabin announced as he pulled the laughing Sam onto his lap.

"Dad! I'm too big to sit on your lap," Sam protested—but only a little.

Mr. Sabin gave Sam a quick hug. "Since when?"

"Since last year. I'm in junior high, you know!" Sam said, laughing as she jumped off her dad's lap.

"They grow up so fast," Mr. Sabin shook his head sadly. "Hey! where are you going?" he asked as Sam pushed through the swinging doors that separated the kitchen from the dining room.

"Upstairs," Sam yelled back, "to practice being

Here's Looking at You

beautiful! And if Carrie Yetter calls, tell her I went to have plastic surgery!"

"Plastic what?" Mr. Sabin exclaimed from below.

"Never mind," Sam laughed, happy to have her old face back. "It's just a joke."

"They grow up so fast," Mr. Sabin repeated as he bit into his pastrami sandwich.

Sam's prayer: *Dear God, sometimes I take myself too seriously. Help me learn to laugh at myself more often. And God, is there anything you can do about Carrie Yetter's sense of humor? Amen.*

Action idea: Next time you feel like getting mad, laugh—and see what happens.